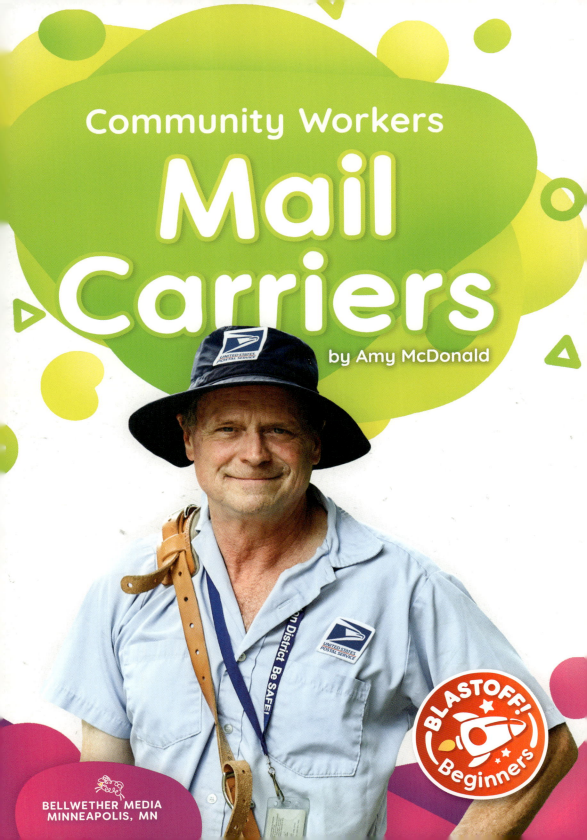

Community Workers
Mail Carriers

by Amy McDonald

BELLWETHER MEDIA • MINNEAPOLIS, MN

BLASTOFF! Beginners

Blastoff! Beginners are developed by literacy experts and educators to meet the needs of early readers. These engaging informational texts support young children as they begin reading about their world. Through simple language and high frequency words paired with crisp, colorful photos, Blastoff! Beginners launch young readers into the universe of independent reading.

Sight Words in This Book

a	have	the
at	in	they
each	it	up
for	so	who
get	some	

This edition first published in 2025 by Bellwether Media, Inc.

No part of this publication may be reproduced in whole or in part without written permission of the publisher. For information regarding permission, write to Bellwether Media, Inc., Attention: Permissions Department, 6012 Blue Circle Drive, Minnetonka, MN 55343.

Library of Congress Cataloging-in-Publication Data

Names: McDonald, Amy, 1985- author.
Title: Mail carriers / by Amy McDonald.
Description: Minneapolis, MN : Bellwether Media, Inc., 2025. | Series: Blastoff! beginners: community workers | Includes bibliographical references and index. | Audience: Ages 4-7 | Audience: Grades K-1 |
Identifiers: LCCN 2024004953 (print) | LCCN 2024004954 (ebook) | ISBN 9798886870091 (library binding) | ISBN 9781644878460 (ebook)
Subjects: LCSH: Letter carriers--Juvenile literature. | Postal service--Juvenile literature.
Classification: LCC HE6241 .M395 2025 (print) | LCC HE6241 (ebook) | DDC 383/.145--dc23/eng/20240202
LC record available at https://lccn.loc.gov/2024004953
LC ebook record available at https://lccn.loc.gov/2024004954

Text copyright © 2025 by Bellwether Media, Inc. BLASTOFF! BEGINNERS and associated logos are trademarks and/or registered trademarks of Bellwether Media, Inc. Bellwether Media is a division of Chrysalis Education Group.

Editor: Betsy Rathburn   Designer: Laura Sowers

Printed in the United States of America, North Mankato, MN.

Table of Contents

On the Job	4
What Are They?	6
What Do They Do?	12
Why Do We Need Them?	20
Mail Carrier Facts	22
Glossary	23
To Learn More	24
Index	24

On the Job

Who works in rain or snow? Mail carriers!

What Are They?

Mail carriers **deliver** mail. They work for the post office.

post office

They work
in cities.
They work
in small towns.

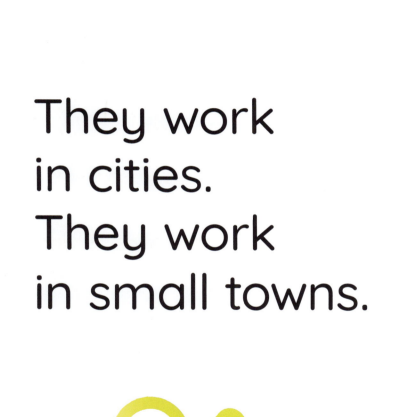

They wear **uniforms**.
They have hats.
They have jackets.

jacket

What Do They Do?

Mail carriers bring letters. They bring **packages**.

packages

They pick up mail.
It gets **sorted**.

Some walk.
They carry a bag.

Some drive a truck.
They stop at each mailbox.

Why Do We Need Them?

So much mail! Mail carriers bring it!

Mail Carrier Facts

Tools

bag

uniform

truck

A Day in the Life

deliver letters

deliver packages

pick up mail

Glossary

deliver

to bring

packages

boxes that hold items

sorted

put in groups based on where it will go

uniforms

outfits worn by workers

To Learn More

ON THE WEB

FACTSURFER

Factsurfer.com gives you a safe, fun way to find more information.

1. Go to www.factsurfer.com.

2. Enter "mail carriers" into the search box and click 🔍.

3. Select your book cover to see a list of related content.

Index

bag, 16, 17
cities, 8
deliver, 6
drive, 18
hats, 10, 11
jackets, 10
letters, 12
mail, 6, 14, 20

mailbox, 18
packages, 12
post office, 6
rain, 4
snow, 4
sorted, 14
towns, 8
truck, 18

uniforms, 10
walk, 16
works, 4, 6, 8

The images in this book are reproduced through the courtesy of: EyeWolf/ Getty Images, front cover; ten43, p. 3; Bloomberg/ Contributor/ Getty Images, pp. 4-5, 10-11, 16-17; Althom, p. 6 (post office); Handout/ Handout/ Getty Images, pp. 6-7; Bastiaan Slabbers, pp. 8-9; Justin Sullivan/ Staff/ Getty Images, p. 10 (jacket); Bobkov Evgeniy, p. 12 (packages); Jim West/ Alamy, pp. 12-13; imagean, pp. 14-15; New Africa, p. 18; Images-USA/ Alamy, pp. 18-19; UPI/ Alamy, pp. 20-21; Keith Homan, p. 22 (bag); Dzha33, p. 22 (uniform); cleanfotos, p. 22 (truck); Paul Matzner/ Alamy, p. 22 (deliver letters); Irfan Khan/ Contributor/ Getty Images, p. 22 (deliver packages); David R. Frazier Photolibrary, Inc./ Alamy, p. 22 (pick up mail); Jillian Cain Photography, p. 23 (deliver); Roschetzky Photography, p. 23 (packages); Krysja, p. 23 (sorted); Joe Raedle, p. 23 (uniform).